# YOUR KNOWLEDGE HAS VALUE

# The economic value of data in the 21st century

Anke Wiards

**Bibliographic information published by the German National Library:**

The German National Library lists this publication in the National Bibliography; detailed bibliographic data are available on the Internet at http://dnb.dnb.de.

ISBN: 9783346580665
This book is also available as an ebook.

Print and binding: Books on Demand GmbH, Norderstedt, Germany
Printed on acid-free paper from responsible sources.

The present work has been carefully prepared. Nevertheless, authors and publishers do not incur liability for the correctness of information, notes, links and advice as well as any printing errors.

GRIN web shop: https://www.grin.com/document/1167782

# The economic value of data
## Data as the oil of the 21 centuries?

Economics and law

*15.12.2021*

# Table of contents

# Bibliography

**Ballsun-Stanton,**
Brian

Asking about data: experimental philosophy of information technology,
5th Edition, Sydney 30.12.2010, pp. 119-224;

*quoted as: Ballsun-Stanton, Asking about data.*

**Bründl,** Simon
**Matt,** Christian
**Hess,** Thomas

Wertschöpfung in Datenmärkten eine explorative Untersuchung am
Beispiel des deutschen Marktes für persönliche Daten,
Munich, 14.12.2021;

*quoted as: Br/Ma/He, value creation in data markets, page.*

**Danciu,** Radu
**Deac,** Marius

Issues Related to the accounting treatment of the tangible and intangible
assets depreiation,
Oradea 20.02.2011,
Economic Science Series, Edition 20, No.2, pp. 498-502,

*quoted as: Da/De, ESS, page.*

**Hinterhölzl,** Klara

„Einstiegen" in die Welt der Wirtschaft,
12th Austrian Business Education Congress,

*quoted as: Hinterhölzl, 12th ABEC, „Getting in" to the world of business.*

**Kleinaltenkamp,**
Michael

Handwörterbuch des ökonomischen Systems der Bundesrepublik Deutsch-
lands,
Wiesbaden 2005, pp. 218-222;

*quoted as: Kleinaltenkamp, Principles of economics, page.*

**Lapp,** Jennifer

Die interessantesten Google-Statistiken aus dem vergangenen Jahr,
https://blog.hubspot.de/marketing/google-trends-suche
28.12.2020,

*quoted as: Google statistic, access of data.*

**Lichtenauer,** Thomas

Was sind persönliche Daten Wert?
Entwicklung eines Artefakts zur Ermittlung der optimalen Methode zur
Bewertung von persönlichen Daten,
Juli 2020,

*quoted as: Lichtenauer, What is the value of personal data? (page).*

**Lüttringhaus,**
Jan

Das internationale Datenprivatrecht: Baustein des Wirtschaftskolli-
sionsrechts des 21. Jahrhunderts,

ZVglRWiss 117 (2018) 50-82,

*quoted as: Luettringhaus, ZVglRWiss 117 (2018) pp. 50-82, page.*

**Maleri,** Rudolf

Grundlagen der Dienstleistungsproduktion,

3. Edition, Heidelberg 1994;

*quoted as: Maleri, Fundamentals of service production, page.*

**Matschke,**
Manfred Jürgen
**Brösel,** Gerrit

Unternehmensbewertung: Funktionen – Methoden – Grundsätze,

4. Edition, Wiesbaden 2013,

*quoted as: Ma/Br, Business valuation, page.*

**Merkel,** Angela

Datenstrategie in enger europäischer Zusammenarbeit,

The German Federal Gouvernement,

Video Podcast, 08.02.2020,

*quoted as: Data strategy in close European cooperation, date of access, time.*

**Rabe,** Lena

Anzahl der Visits von amazon.de von März 2019 bis -november 2021,

09.12.2021,

https://de.statista.com/statistik/daten/studie/995588/umfrage/anzahl-der-
visits-pro-monat-von-amazonde/

*quoted as: Amazon statistc, access of data.*

**Rudy,** Lisa Jo

*Tangible vs. Intangible Assets: What's the Difference,*

*27.08.2021, the balance*

*https://www.thebalance.com/tangible-vs-intangible-assets-5199067,*

*quoted as: Rudy, Tangible vs. Intangible Assets, date of access.*

**Social and Economic**
**Data Council**

Datenerhebung mit neuer Informationstechnologie

Empfehlungen zu Datenqualität und -management, Forschungsethik und
Datenschutz,

RatSWD Output, No. 6 (6) 2020, pp. 6-38,

*quoted as: SED, Data collection with new information technology, RatSWD Output, No. 6 (6) 2020, (page);*

**Statista Research Department**  Anzahl der monatlich aktiven Facebook Nutzer weltweit vom 1. Quartal 2009 bis zum 3. Quartal 2021,

28.10.2021,

https://de.statista.com/statistik/daten/studie/37545/umfrage/anzahl-der-aktiven-nutzer-von-facebook/

*quoted as: Facebook statistic, access of data.*

**Weicher,** Thilo  Big Data und Datenschutz,

Unabhängiges Landeszentrum für Datenschutz Schleswig-Holstein,

18.03.2018,

*quoted as: Weichert, Big Data und Datenschutz, Structure;*

**Wohlgemuth,** Oliver  Möglichkeiten zur Übertragung verwandter Ansätze auf das Netzwerkcontrolling,
**Hess,** Thomas

No. 1, Goettingen 1999,

*quoted as: Wo/He, Possibilities for transferring related approaches to network controlling, page.*

**Wöhrmann,** Arnt  Immaterielle Güter,

Wiesbaden 2009, pp. 11-15,

*quoted as: Wöhrmann, intangible Impairment, page.*

**Criddle,** Cristina  Facebook sued over Cambridge Analytica data scandal,

BBC News, 28.10.2020,

*quoted as: Criddle, Facebook sued over Cambridge Analytica data scandal, date of access.*

# List of figures/tables

# A.  Introduction

*"Data is the raw material of the future."*
*- Angela Merkel[1]*

*"Data is just like oil."*
*- Clive Humby[2]*

Data - a term that is no longer unknown in today's age. Rather, they seem to be everywhere, data is collected everywhere in our everyday lives. From the supermarket around the corner to banks to doctor's visits, data is collected everywhere. With the help of new information technology, smartphones, wearables such as watches and other sensors, data collection is being given a whole new reach. Data is collected from the user everywhere and at all times. What is happening around us, where are we going, what time of day are we out and about, who or what are we spending our time with, all this is data that is collected in real time and then analysed. The business with this data is also no longer unknown. Big names like Google, Facebook and Amazon are common. To give a clue to the whole idea: Google is said to have about 2 trillion users a year. Facebook can boast 2.91 billion users in the third quarter of 2021 and Amazon has 548 million active customer accounts so far this year.[3]

# B.  Calculation of value

## I.  How do you measure the economic value of data?

How do you measure the value of something you cannot touch? What can neither be weighed nor physically measured? This question is particularly important with regard to the product "data".

## 1.  Data as a Product

Data are intangible products. Intangible products can initially be generally recognised products such as works of literature, art or science. Furthermore, products such as designs or trademarks

---

[1] Data strategy in close European cooperation, 14.12.2021, 0:31min;
[2] Humby, teaching at Kellogg School of Management in 2006, http://ana.blogs.com/maestros/2006/11/data_is_the_new.html - 15.12.2021;
[3] Amazon statistic, 13.12.2021; Facebook statistic 13.12.2021; Google statistic 13.12.2021; *SED,* Data collection with new information technology, RatSWD Output, No. 6 (6) 2020, (7);

are protected. However, intangible products also include general information, data, know-how and references.[4]

But even today, there is no clear definition of data. First of all, it should be said that in the literature there is no real difference between the term "data" and "information", both are more or less the same.[5]

Brian Ballsun-Stanton distinguished data into three terms:

(1) Data can be facts that are objective, reproducible results of measurements and make true statements about reality. This term is widely used in the natural sciences.

(2) Data can be the result of observation. They then represent a recorded perception, which in turn requires contextual knowledge and filtering or refinement. For example, a person's notes, au-dio and video recordings.

(3) The last idea sees data as binary messages, i.e. signs that serve communication. According to this idea, they can be in the form of texts, diagrams or tables.[6]

Accordingly, data are signs, strings, indications, (numerical) values or knowledge. The author believes that data is additionally and above all a product of the human mind.

Compared to tangible goods, they have many differences, which are compared in the following table.

| Data/tangible goods | Intangible goods |
| --- | --- |
| Tangible goods show wear and tear after use. They are therefore consumed. This in turn results in the product losing value (example: value new and used cars).[7] | Intangible data are almost not consumed. After it has been processed, the data can still provide the same information in the same way. Thus, they lose virtually no value through processing.[8] |

---

[4] *Wöhrmann,* intangible Impairment, p. 3ff.; *Maleri,* Fundamentals of service production, p. 9; *Ma/Br,* Business valuation, 123;
[5] *Wöhrmann,* intangible Impairment, p. 11;
[6] *Ballsun-Stanton,* Asking about data;
[7] *Kleinaltenkamp,* Principles of economics, p. 222; *Rudy,* Tangible vs. Intangible Assets, 31.11.2021; *Da/De,* ESS, p. 499;
[8] *Rudy,* Tangible vs. Intangible Assets, 31.11.2021;

As already noted, material goods show signs of wear and tear or they are completely consumed.[9]

A knife, for example, often loses its sharp blade after repeated use; this represents the closure of the product.

If five out of ten pieces of wood are thrown into the fireplace for heating, 50 % are consumed.

Data neither wears out nor is consumed. Several processors can use the same data at the same time and for the same purpose and still make a profit. The processing of one does not diminish the processing value of the other. The data does not lose substance or function.[10]

The duplication of a tangible product is usually equal to the cost of its original acquisition. It is usually not possible to duplicate it at all.[11]

Data can be produced at will, copied cheaply and duplicated, which is another reason why it loses almost no value after use.[12]

Mineral, metallic and fossil raw materials do not renew themselves. In the long term, this, combined with population growth and the resulting increase in demand, leads to a shortage of resources. This ultimately determines our entire economic thinking. The scarcer a resource is, the more its value increases.[13]

Data arise as a product of human existence. In the author's view, they represent information that finds its origin in the human thought system. As long as there are people, there will also be data. A scarcity of resources is thus ruled out and the basic principle of our economy is circumvented.[14]

This comparison clearly shows how different tangible and intangible products are. Nevertheless, business generally applies three approaches to determining the value of tangible goods to intangible ones. In an abstract way, they are supposed to enable the calculation of the data value.[15]

---

[9] *Da/De*, ESS, p. 498;

[10] *Da/De*, ESS, p. 499;

[11] *Maleri*, Fundamentals of service production, p. 3;

[12] *Wöhrmann*, intangible Impairment, p. 14; *Maleri*, Fundamentals of service production, p. 3;

[13] *Kleinaltenkamp*, Principles of economics, P. 222;

[14] *Hinterhölzl*, 12th ABEC, "Getting in" to the world of business;

[15] *Lichtenauer,* What is the value of personal data? (32); *Br/Ma/He,* value creation in data markets, p. 11; *Rudy,* Tangible vs. Intangible Assets, 31.11.2021;

## 2.        Cost-based approach

Starting with the cost approach. Here the company asks itself what costs have I actually incurred? What costs are incurred in holding the product? The costs of purchasing, production,
maintenance and costs that arise when the company makes data available to third parties are
considered here.[16]

## 3.        The value of use

The second approach to be presented is that of the value in use.

The value in use approach is ultimately measured by the savings that the company receives
through the use of the data. This can be imagined as follows:

A company stores and
regularly updates data
from its regular suppli-
ers. It creates a file in
which it stores all the
data it has already col-
lected and will add all
future data.

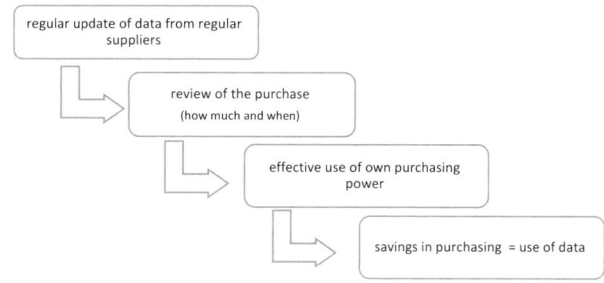

This structure, or rather this file, enables the company to track exactly when it bought what
quantity and at what price.

With this knowledge, the company can consciously use its purchasing power. Based on the data
analysed from its own database, the company can renegotiate prices and negotiate new contract
terms. The resulting difference corresponds to the value of the file.

In this way, the company can save on purchasing. This difference makes up the value of the
data.[17]

## 4.    Market value approach

The last approach to be presented is that of market value. In the context of this, the company
asks itself who its buyer actually is and what the buyer would be willing to pay.

---

[16] *Ma/Br,* Business valuation, 16f.; *Wo/He*, Possibilities for transferring related approaches to network controlling,
p. 15;
[17] *Da/De*, ESS, p. 500; *Maleri*, Fundamentals of service production, p. 71ff;

Here, too, there are different groups of buyers, but the greatest difference in value results from the purchase of raw data or already analysed data, also known as refined data. Raw data is usually cheaper because it has not yet been analysed. The context or the analysis of the data is missing. For example, if a company buys a location file from a user, the company knows when the user was where, but it lacks any context such as length of stay or how often the user visits that location.

Sophisticated data already includes this context. The buyer thus saves on working time, but not on information content.[18]

## II.  Intended use and user

Furthermore, a distinction must be made between the respective users and their purposes of use. There are several actors in data processing; in more detail, we will focus primarily on companies and secondarily on the state.

As already mentioned, companies buy raw or refined data. They want to trade with the data. The main use here is the possibility to create individualised advertisements and content based on the purchased data in order to shape and influence the behaviour or opinion of the user. Particular focus is placed on location, contact and preference data.[19]

The Goverment priority to work with data is to prevent terrorismus and to do law enforcement. To form the opinion companies (like Cambridge Analytics) working with the fears and anxiety. To change the opinion of someone these emotions are the most effective one.

A very well-known case here is that of the company Cambridge Analytics. They were accused of illegal data processing in 2018. In doing so, they unjustifiably accessed thousands probably millions of data of the social media giant Facebook. They used this data to help Donald Trump's election campaign team and that of Brexit are England. They analysed the data and spammed targeted people with election content to win them over to their respective interests. Famously, both turned out positively for their respective supporters: Trump won the presidential election and the Brexit was democratically approved.[20]

---

[18] *Br/Ma/He,* value creation in data markets, 11; *Wo/He,* Possibilities for transferring related approaches to network controlling, p. 13;

[19] *Luettringhaus,* ZVglRWiss 117 (2018) 50-82, 51; *Br/Ma/He,* value creation in data markets, 4;

[20]Criddle, Facebook sued over Cambridge Analytica data scandal 14.12.2021;

### III. How to collect Data

How is the data collected in the first place? This can happen through various methods.

Smartphones, for example, have several sensors:

> the Global Positioning System (GPS), cameras, microphones, accelerometers and log files.

Through apps or so-called cookies, the user can then allow a data processing company to access and process his or her data. This is called tracking. Tracking means the monitoring of measurable human behaviour.[21]

The implementation via apps is quite simple. If the user agrees to the data protection agreements of the app, he also agrees to the tracking conditions with the same "click".

Website providers sell so-called advertising space to other companies. These can place their cookies there. The user accepts the cookies in the form of a visual obstruction. For example, the user wants to read an article or use a website service. The cookies usually visually block a part of the page or deny access completely if the user does not agree to them or as long as the user does not agree to them.

After the page is closed again, one could assume that the tracking has ended. However, this is very often not the case. In most cases, tracking continues even when the page is closed. [22]

The data processing company gets access to almost all activities carried out - via the respective device or profile - by means of accepted cookies. It can access other open pages or apps and the activity that takes place there.

For the data processing company, there is thus almost no restriction on access to personal data.

### IV. What makes personal data so valuable?

It is now clear how data are collected and what purpose is pursued with their processing. But why is personal data so valuable?

Many Internet platforms live from the fact that users who use their services "free of charge" disclose certain private data in return, which the platform operator can use for its own commercial purposes or sell on to data-processing companies. [23]

---

[21] *SED,* Data collection with new information technology, RatSWD Output, No. 6 (6) 2020, (8f.); *Br/Ma/He,* value creation in data markets, 6; *Weichert,* Big Data und Datenschutz, 6. Stages of data processing;

[22] *Br/Ma/He,* value creation in data markets, 6;

[23] *Haberstumpf,* Verkauf immaterieller Güter, NJOZ 2015, 793 (794);

## 1.    Facebook

One of the best-known companies here is Facebook.

The following is a list of what information/data is tracked from the user via proprietary tools. The list is not exhaustive. It is only an insight into the possibilities of Facebook.

Facebook tracks:

1. all information from all devices connected to the internet, as well as

2. all app and document names and their respective document type that are on the affected device

3. information about nearby Wi-Fi hotspots and cell towers to narrow down and pinpoint the user's location

4. information about other nearby devices or devices that are on the same network to identify and classify social contacts

5. purchases you make on non-Facebook sites, such as Amazon, eBay, Nike, etc.

6. all contact information, including the user's address book if the user has linked it

7. location and date of a photo taken by the user. Facebook pulls this information from the image's metadata

8. the device number of your smartphone or installed games and apps, this is the so-called identification options

9. interactions with friends, what the user shares with them

10. comments, likes and reactions

Based on all this data, Facebook can create a user profile that shows personal characteristics, preferences, strengths and weaknesses. With the help of this knowledge, buying behaviour can be influenced. This goal is pursued with the placement of individual content and advertisements.[24]

By refining the raw data, it can be linked to other circumstances.

Companies can explicitly select their target audience, tailor advertising to age groups, preferences or needs and thus be more effective and ultimately less expensive. This is what makes data so valuable.

How profitable this type of use is can also be seen in the example of Facebook.

In 2020, the company will generate 97% of its revenue from advertising.

---

[24] *Luettringhaus,* ZVglRWiss 117 (2018) 50-82, 54;

The company's turnover in 2020 was 86 billion US dollars.[25] In the same year, they had a user base of 2.3 billion. If you divide the 86 billion by 2.3 billion, you get a value of 37.40 dollars. This corresponds to the value per user file. It is pointed out that the user makes this data available without asking for payment.

## 2.    Excursive statement question

Imagine a library. It is open at all times and contains all kinds of information. By consenting to the processing of our data, we open a digital library. Open at any time with all information - about us. Origin information, eating habits, professional history, personal history, pets, siblings, where we live, which bars and restaurants we visit, who our friends are and what we don't like. We provide all this data free of charge for third parties to read, influence and recruit us.
If they think about it, are you okay with that?

## 3.    Example: Hanna

The following example illustrates how far-reaching or how such a data analysis can be:
Hanna is 34 years old. She has been with Markus since 2013. They both like to visit the bar across the street and often host wine tasting evenings with their friends, in Hanna's flat.
For the past seven weeks, however, Hanna has stopped going to the bar, her online purchases have changed from wine to smoothies, and she uses various search engines to look for safe environments and good day-care centres. In addition, she now stops for three seconds longer than usual when looking at baby photos.
The data processing company concludes that Hanna wants to have a baby or is already pregnant. As a result, she now receives content and advertisements about pregnancy and children. Flat advertisements are also included, since a new addition to the family often entails a "change of scenery".

---

[25]https://de.statista.com/statistik/daten/studie/217061/umfrage/umsatz-gewinn-von-facebook-weltweit/, 27.11.2021;

## 4. Development of digital advertising market

The statistics from "*statisa digital market outlook*" from 2021 show the development of the digital advertising market.

In the area of search, digital advertising grew by 57.11 %.

In the area of social media, the growth was 80.44 %. Significant increases were also recorded in the context of the other

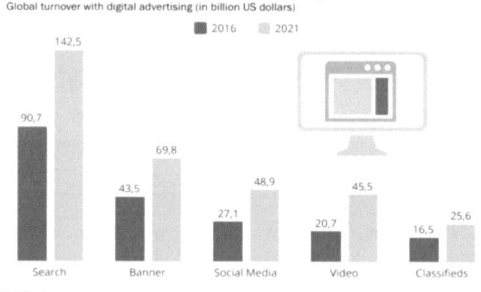

**Development of the digital advertising market**
Global turnover with digital advertising (in billion US dollars)

three areas. Ultimately, one can say that the digital advertising market is in constant growth.

## C. Conclusion

Based on the facts just presented, the author concludes that the user is not the customer, but the product.

Companies use their almost unlimited access to data to collect huge amounts of information about people. They analyse this in ways that the average user cannot comprehend. They filter out fears, desires, likes, dislikes and current life circumstances, correlate them and present their "individualised" products and services to the user.

And the business with knowledge about the inner life of a person seems to be one of the most profitable in the world, because the data we leave behind establishes an industry that generates a turnover of 100 million.

The industry market volume of digital advertising is even expected to rise to € 382,039 million in 2021.

Data can therefore be described as the oil of the 21st century.

# YOUR KNOWLEDGE HAS VALUE